BEHIND THE SCENES BIOGRAPHIES

T0008799

WHAT YOU NEVER KNEW ABOUT

DEMI LOVATO

by Helen Cox Cannons

CAPSTONE PRESS
a capstone imprint

This is an unauthorized biography.

Published by Spark, an imprint of Capstone
1710 Roe Crest Drive, North Mankato, Minnesota 56003
capstonepub.com

Library of Congress Cataloging-in-Publication Data is available on the Library of Congress website.

ISBN: 9781666356908 (hardcover)
ISBN: 9781669040132 (paperback)
ISBN: 9781666356915 (ebook PDF)

Summary: Young readers learn behind-the-scenes facts and exciting details about actor-turned-singer Demi Lovato.

Editorial Credits
Editor: Mandy Robbins; Designer: Heidi Thompson; Media Researcher: Jo Miller; Production Specialist: Tori Abraham

Image Credits
Alamy: REUTERS, 10, WENN US, 23; Associated Press: Chris Pizzello, Cover; Getty Images: Brandon Williams, 14, HIGHFIVE/Bauer-Griffin, 18, JB Lacroix, 16, Kevin Mazur, 20, Kevin Mazur, 21, Rich Fury, 27, SXSW, 28; Shutterstock: Cristian Dina, 13, DFree, 7 (right), DoctorIce Photography, 7 (left), Everett Collection, 24, (left), Kathy Hutchins, 24 (right), Lightspring, 8 (left), maRRitch, 9 (bottom), Minii Ho, 27 (inset), peiyang, 17, sbw18, 15, Simple Line, 9 (top), Sky Cinema, 4, 12, Steve Collender, 8 (right), Tinseltown, 26, VectorPlotnikoff, 19

All internet sites appearing in back matter were available and accurate when this book was sent to press.

Printed and bound in the USA. PO5195

TABLE OF CONTENTS

Words in **bold** are in the glossary.

A GLOBAL **STAR**

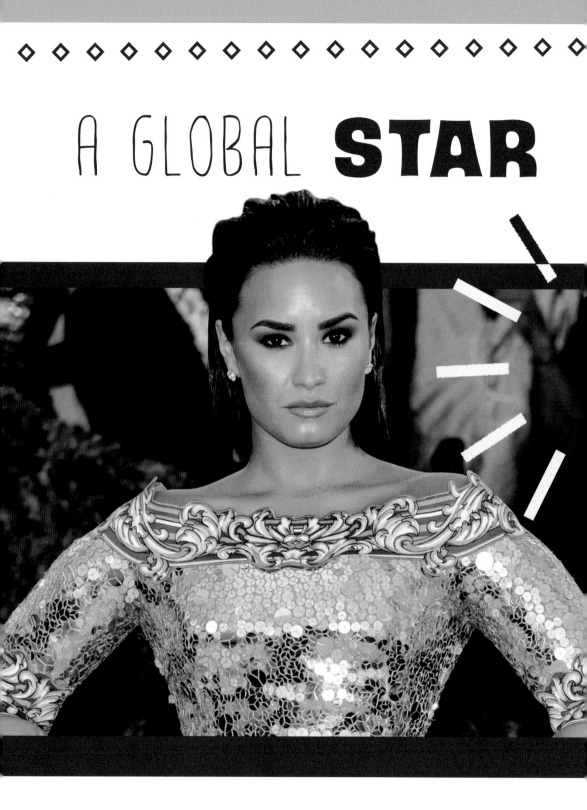

Are you "Sorry Not Sorry" for loving Demi Lovato? They're a global star. They are also an **LGBTQ+ icon**. But did you know that their first name isn't Demi? It's Demetria.

What else is there to know about Demi? Read on to find out!

DEMI'S
DELIGHTS

Do you call yourself a Lovatic?

Do you know their:

1.   **Favorite food?**

2.   **Star sign?**

3.   **Favorite colors?**

4.   **Favorite type of music?**

5.   **Musical instruments they can play?**

FACT
Demi uses the pronouns "they" and "their." They are **nonbinary**. That means they don't identify with only being male or female.

1. Taco Bell **2.** Leo **3.** Black and red

4. Heavy metal **5.** Drums, guitar, and piano

What does Demi do when
they're not performing? They surf
and play volleyball.

✖ ✖ ✖ ✖ ✖ ✖ ✖ ✖ ✖ ✖ ✖ ✖ ✖ ✖ ✖ ✖

✖ ✖ ✖ ✖ ✖ ✖ ✖ ✖ ✖ ✖ ✖ ✖ ✖ ✖ ✖

They also do Brazilian **jiujitsu**.
In August 2017, Demi got their
blue belt.

"*I think it's really cool to learn
something that helps you with
self-defense.*"
—Demi Lovato (*Self*, August 16, 2017)

DEMI
BY THE NUMBERS

Check out the "Confident" star's most important numbers.

Demetria Devonne Lovato was born August 20, 1992. Their first acting role was on the TV show *Barney & Friends*. They were 10 years old. They have won 14 Teen Choice Awards.

FACT

One of Demi's nicknames is McD Love.

Demi's numbers prove they are a rock star. They have sold more than 2.7 million albums. Their songs have had 23.8 million **downloads**.

2.7

Demi has big numbers on social media too. They have 127 million Instagram followers and growing. More than 54 million people follow them on Twitter too.

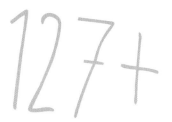

FACT
Demi is also a movie star. They starred in two Camp Rock movies.

WE ARE
FAMILY

left to right:
Demi's stepfather Eddie, Demi, their sisters
Dallas and Madison, and mom Dianna

Demi has a tight-knit family. Their father, Patrick, died in 2003. They are very close to their mom, Dianna. Demi's stepfather, Eddie, has supported them on tour. He was their manager for a while.

FACT
Demi says they got their singing voice from their mom.

Did you know Demi has three sisters? Dallas is four years older than Demi. Demi's younger half sister is actor Madison De La Garza. Demi also has an older half sister named Amber. Demi was 20 when they met Amber!

Madison De La Garza

Demi wanted to know what their **ancestry** was. They took a **DNA** test. Check out what it said!

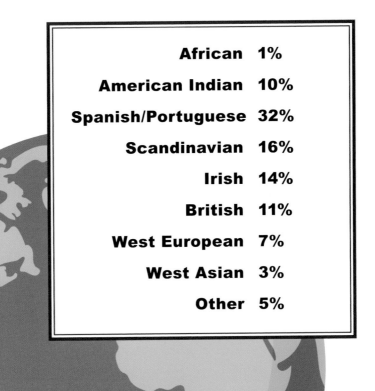

African	1%
American Indian	10%
Spanish/Portuguese	32%
Scandinavian	16%
Irish	14%
British	11%
West European	7%
West Asian	3%
Other	5%

PUPPY **LOVE!**

Batman

What else does Demi love besides their family? Their dogs! Batman and Cinderella are tiny dogs, but they once stopped a **burglary**. In 2017, a man tried to break into Demi's house. He climbed up a ladder. The dogs barked and the burglar ran away.

FAMOUS FRIENDS
AND FEUDS

Miley Cyrus

Miley Cyrus is a good friend of Demi's. They were both Disney Channel stars. Miley calls Demi when they need someone to talk to.

Ariana Grande

Demi is also good friends with Ariana Grande. Both were child actors before becoming pop stars. Ariana sang on Demi's **single**, "Met Him Last Night."

"Ariana is one that's always gonna be there."
—Demi Lovato (*Teen Vogue*, April 4, 2021)

Demi used to be close with Selena Gomez. They starred together in *Barney & Friends*. They were Disney Channel stars together too. They're not such good friends now. Rumor has it that Demi thought Taylor Swift stole their friend away. Ouch!

FACT

Demi and Selena used to have matching guitar-pick necklaces.

Selena Gomez

DEMI'S
CHANGING STYLE

2008

2013

Demi's style has changed a lot in the last 10 years. In their Camp Rock days, they had a sweet look. They wore their hair long, with bangs.

In the mid-2010s, Demi's look was much more edgy. They had short hair. They started dyeing it different colors.

2018

In the late 2010s and early 2020s, Demi's hair was slicked back. They wore long, sweeping dresses.

In December 2021, Demi shaved their head. They wanted a fresh start. They came out as nonbinary.

2021

BEST EFFORTS

Demi tries to be a good role model. They have talked about their mental health struggles. They have spoken out against bullying. They are a proud member of the LGBTQ+ community. They also work with many groups to help people.

"Every day we wake up, we are given another opportunity and chance to be who we want and wish to be."
—Demi Lovato (Twitter, May 19, 2021)

Glossary

ancestry (AN-sess-tree)—relating to family members who lived a long time ago

burglary (BURG-lur-ree)—the act of breaking into a building to steal things

DNA—genetic information in the cells of plants and animals; DNA is short for deoxyribonucleic acid

download (DOUN-lohd)—music, or other type of file, that is transferred onto an electronic device such as a cellphone or computer

icon (EYE-kon)—a person who is very successful and admired by many

jiujitsu (joo-JIT-soo)—a type of Japanese martial art

LGBTQ+—stands for lesbian, gay, bisexual, transgender, queer (or sometimes questioning), and others

nonbinary (non-BI-nayr-ee)—having a gender identity that is neither male nor female

single (SING-guhl)—one song from an album; often played on the radio to get a new album noticed

Read More

Bach, Greg. *Ariana Grande*. Hollywood: Mason Crest, 2022.

Neuenfeldt, Elizabeth. *Selena Gomez: Mental Health Advocate*. Minneapolis: Bellweather Media, Inc., 2022.

Terp, Gail. *Demi Lovato*. Mankato, MN: Black Rabbit Books, 2017.

Internet Sites

Demi Lovato: Official Site
demilovato.com

Demi Lovato Tells Becky G How Meditation Helped Them Realize They Were Non-Binary
etonline.com/demi-lovato-tells-becky-g-how-meditation-helped-them-realize-they-were-non-binary-exclusive-174751

People.com: Demi Lovato
people.com/tag/demi-lovato/

Index

About the Author

Helen Cox Cannons was born in Dumfriesshire, Scotland. She has a Master's Degree in English Literature from the University of Edinburgh. She has worked as an editor and author for over 25 years. In her spare time, Helen likes to crochet, sing, go for country walks, and fuss over her two cats, Nero and Diego. She lives in Witney, Oxfordshire, with her two daughters, Abby and Serena.